forget me not

❧ ✿ ❧

DIETER F. UCHTDORF

DESERET
BOOK

SALT LAKE CITY, UTAH

Adapted from Dieter F. Uchtdorf, "Forget Me Not," *Ensign,* November 2011, 120–23.

Art direction by Richard Erickson.
Cover and interior design by Sheryl Dickert Smith.
Production design by Kayla Hackett.
Cover and interior illustrations from Shutterstock, Thinkstock, and iStock.

© 2012 Dieter F. Uchtdorf

Visit us at DeseretBook.com

(CIP on file)
ISBN 978-1-60907-119-6

Printed in the United States of America
Publishers Printing, Salt Lake City, UT
10   9   8   7   6   5   4   3   2   1

contents

A while ago I was walking through a beautiful garden with my wife and daughter. I marveled at the glory and beauty of God's creation. And then I noticed, among all the glorious blooms, the tiniest flower. I knew the name of this flower because since I was a child I have had a tender connection to it.

THE FLOWER IS CALLED

forget-me-not.

I'm not exactly sure why this tiny flower has meant so much to me over the years. It does not attract immediate attention; it is easy to overlook among larger and more vibrant flowers; yet it is just as beautiful, with its rich color that mirrors that of the bluest skies—perhaps this is one reason why I like it so much.

AND THERE IS THE HAUNTING PLEA OF ITS NAME.

There is a German legend that just as God had finished naming all the plants, one was left unnamed. A tiny voice spoke out,

"Forget me not, O Lord!"

And God replied that this would be its name.

I would like to use
this little flower as a metaphor.
The five petals of the little
forget-me-not flower prompt me
to consider five things we would
be wise never to forget.

FIRST,

forget not to be patient

with yourself.

I want to tell you something that I hope you will take in the right way: God is fully aware that you and I are not perfect.

Let me add: God is also fully aware that the people you think are perfect are not.

And yet we spend so much time and energy comparing ourselves to others—usually comparing our weaknesses to their strengths. This drives us to create expectations for ourselves that are impossible to meet. As a result, we never celebrate our good efforts because they seem to be less than what someone else does.

Everyone has strengths and weaknesses. It's wonderful that you have strengths. And it is part of your mortal experience that you do have weaknesses.

God wants to help us

to eventually turn all of our weaknesses into strengths,[1]

but He knows that this is a long-term goal.

HE WANTS US TO BECOME PERFECT,[2]

and if we stay on the path of discipleship, one day we will.

It's okay that you're not quite there yet.

Keep working on it, but

STOP PUNISHING YOURSELF.

Dear sisters, many of you are endlessly compassionate and patient with the weaknesses of others. Please remember also to be compassionate and patient with yourself.

*I*n the meantime, be thankful
for all the small successes in your home,
your family relationships, your education and livelihood,
your Church participation and personal improvement. Like
the forget-me-nots, these successes may seem tiny to you and
they may go unnoticed by others, but God notices them and
they are not small to Him. If you consider success to be only
the most perfect rose or dazzling orchid, you may miss some
of life's sweetest experiences.

or example, insisting that you have a picture-perfect family home evening each week—even though doing so makes you and everyone around you miserable—may not be the best choice. Instead, ask yourself, "What could we do as a family that would be enjoyable and spiritual and bring us closer together?" That family home evening—though it may be modest in scope and execution—may have far more positive long-term results.

OUR JOURNEY TOWARD PERFECTION IS LONG,

BUT WE CAN FIND WONDER AND DELIGHT IN EVEN

THE TINIEST STEPS IN THAT JOURNEY.

SECOND,

forget not the difference

between a good sacrifice and

a foolish sacrifice.

An acceptable sacrifice is
when we give up something
good for something of far
greater worth.

*G*iving up a little sleep to help a child who is having a nightmare is a good sacrifice. We all know this. Staying up all night, jeopardizing our own health, to make the perfect accessory for a daughter's Sunday outfit may not be such a good sacrifice.

Dedicating some of our time to studying the scriptures or preparing to teach a lesson is a good sacrifice. Spending many hours stitching the title of the lesson into homemade pot holders for each member of your class perhaps may not be.

EVERY PERSON AND SITUATION IS DIFFERENT,

AND A GOOD SACRIFICE IN ONE INSTANCE MIGHT

BE A FOOLISH SACRIFICE IN ANOTHER.

How can we tell the difference for our own situation? We can ask ourselves, "Am I committing my time and energies to the things that matter most?" There are so many good things to do, but we can't do all of them. Our Heavenly Father is most pleased when we sacrifice something good for something far greater with an eternal perspective. Sometimes, that may even mean nurturing small but beautiful forget-me-not flowers instead of a large garden of exotic blooms.

THIRD,

forget not to be

happy now.

In the beloved children's story *Charlie and the Chocolate Factory*, the mysterious candy maker Willy Wonka hides a golden ticket in five of his candy bars and announces that whoever finds one of the tickets wins a tour of his factory and a lifetime supply of chocolate.

Written on each golden ticket is this message: "Greetings to you, the lucky finder of this Golden Ticket . . . ! Tremendous things are in store for you! Many wonderful surprises await you! . . . Mystic and marvelous surprises . . . will . . . delight, . . . astonish, and perplex you."[3]

In this classic children's story, people all over the world desperately yearn to find a golden ticket. Some feel that their entire future happiness depends on whether or not a golden ticket falls into their hands. In their anxiousness, people begin to forget the simple joy they used to find in a candy bar. The candy bar itself becomes an utter disappointment if it does not contain a golden ticket.

So many people today are waiting for their own golden ticket—the ticket that they believe holds the key to the happiness they have always dreamed about. For some, the golden ticket may be a perfect marriage; for others, a magazine-cover home or perhaps freedom from stress or worry.

THERE IS NOTHING WRONG WITH

RIGHTEOUS YEARNINGS—

we hope and seek after things that are

"virtuous, lovely, *or* of good report *or* praiseworthy."[4]

THE PROBLEM COMES WHEN WE
PUT OUR HAPPINESS ON HOLD AS WE
WAIT FOR SOME FUTURE EVENT—
OUR GOLDEN TICKET—TO APPEAR.

One woman wanted more than anything else to marry a righteous priesthood holder in the temple and be a mother and a wife. She had dreamed about this all her life, and oh, what a wonderful mother and loving wife she would be. Her home would be filled with loving-kindness. Never a bitter word would be spoken. The food would never burn. And her children, instead of hanging out with their friends, would prefer to spend their evenings and weekends with Mom and Dad.

This was her golden ticket. It was the one thing upon which she felt her whole existence depended. It was the one thing in all the world for which she most desperately yearned.

But it never happened. And, as the years went on, she became more and more withdrawn, bitter, and even angry. She could not understand why God would not grant her this righteous desire.

She worked as an elementary school teacher, and being around children all day long simply reminded her that her golden ticket had never appeared. As the years passed she became more disappointed and withdrawn. People didn't like being around her and avoided her whenever they could. She even took her frustration out on the children at school. She found herself losing her temper, and she swung between fits of anger and desperate loneliness.

The tragedy of this story is that this dear woman, in all her disappointment about her golden ticket, failed to notice the blessings she *did* have. She did not have children in her home, but she was surrounded by them in her classroom. She was not blessed with a family, but the Lord had given her an opportunity few people have—the chance to influence for good the lives of hundreds of children and families as a teacher.

The lesson here is that

IF WE SPEND OUR DAYS WAITING FOR

FABULOUS ROSES, WE COULD MISS THE BEAUTY

AND WONDER OF THE TINY FORGET-ME-NOTS

THAT ARE ALL AROUND US.

*T*his is not to say that we should abandon hope or temper our goals. Never stop striving for the best that is within you. Never stop hoping for all of the righteous desires of your heart. But don't close your eyes and hearts to the simple and elegant beauties of each day's ordinary moments that make up a rich, well-lived life.

The happiest people I know are not
those who find their golden ticket; they are
those who, while in pursuit of worthy goals,
discover and treasure the beauty and sweet-
ness of the everyday moments. They are the
ones who, thread by daily thread, weave a
tapestry of gratitude and wonder
throughout their lives. These are they
who are truly happy.

FOURTH,

forget not the *why*

of the gospel.

Sometimes, in the routine of our lives, we unintentionally overlook a vital aspect of the gospel of Jesus Christ, much as one might overlook a beautiful, delicate forget-me-not. In our diligent efforts to fulfill all of the duties and obligations we take on as members of the Church, we sometimes see the gospel as a long list of tasks that we must add to our already impossibly long to-do list, as a block of time that we must somehow fit into our busy schedules. We focus on *what* the Lord wants us to do and *how* we might do it, but we sometimes forget *why*.

THE GOSPEL OF JESUS CHRIST IS NOT AN

OBLIGATION; IT IS A PATHWAY, MARKED

BY OUR LOVING FATHER IN HEAVEN,

LEADING TO HAPPINESS AND PEACE IN

THIS LIFE AND GLORY AND INEXPRESSIBLE

FULFILLMENT IN THE LIFE TO COME.

The gospel

IS A LIGHT

THAT PENETRATES

MORTALITY AND

illuminates the way

BEFORE US.

While understanding the *what* and the *how* of the gospel is necessary, the eternal fire and majesty of the gospel springs from the *why*. When we understand *why* our Heavenly Father has given us this pattern for living, when we remember *why* we committed to making it a foundational part of our lives, the gospel ceases to become a burden and, instead, becomes a joy and a delight. It becomes precious and sweet.

Let us not walk the path
of discipleship with our
eyes on the ground,
thinking only of the tasks
and obligations before us.

*Let us not walk unaware
of the beauty of the glorious
earthly and spiritual landscapes
that surround us.*

SEEK OUT THE MAJESTY,

THE BEAUTY, AND THE

EXHILARATING JOY OF THE

why OF THE GOSPEL

OF JESUS CHRIST.

The *what* and *how* of obedience mark the way and keep us on the right path. The *why* of obedience sanctifies our actions, transforming the mundane into the majestic. It magnifies our small acts of obedience into holy acts of consecration.

FIFTH,

forget not that the

Lord loves you.

$\mathcal{A}$s a child, when I would look at the little forget-me-nots, I sometimes felt a little like that flower—small and insignificant. I wondered if I would be forgotten by my family or by my Heavenly Father.

Years later I can look back on that young boy with tenderness and compassion. And I do know now—

I WAS NEVER FORGOTTEN.

And I know something else:

as an Apostle of our Master, Jesus Christ, I proclaim

with all the certainty and conviction of my heart—

neither are you!

You ARE NOT

FORGOTTEN.

Wherever you are, whatever your circumstances may

be, you are not forgotten. No matter how dark your

days may seem, no matter how insignificant you may

feel, no matter how overshadowed you think you

may be, your Heavenly Father has not forgotten you.

In fact, He loves you with an infinite love.

*J*ust think of it: You are known and remembered by the most majestic, powerful, and glorious Being in the universe! You are loved by the King of infinite space and everlasting time!

He who created and knows the stars

knows you and your name—

you are a daughter of His kingdom.

"When I consider thy heavens, the work of thy fingers,

the moon and the stars, which thou hast ordained;

"What is man, that thou art mindful of him? . . .

"For thou hast made him a little lower than the angels,

and hast crowned him with glory and honour."[5]

GOD LOVES YOU BECAUSE YOU ARE HIS CHILD.

HE LOVES YOU EVEN THOUGH AT TIMES YOU MAY

FEEL LONELY OR MAKE MISTAKES.

The love of God and

the power of the restored gospel

are redemptive and saving.

If you will only allow His divine love into your life,

it can dress any wound, heal any hurt, and

soften any sorrow.

MY DEAR SISTERS,

you are closer to heaven than you suppose.

You ARE DESTINED

FOR MORE THAN YOU CAN

POSSIBLY IMAGINE.

Continue to increase in faith and personal
righteousness. Accept the restored
gospel of Jesus Christ as your way of life.
Cherish the gift of activity in this great and
true Church. Treasure the gift of service in the
blessed organization of Relief Society.
Continue to strengthen homes and families.
Continue to seek out and help others who
need your and the Lord's help.

here is something inspiring and sublime about the little forget-me-not flower. I hope it will be a symbol of the little things that make your lives joyful and sweet. Please never forget that you must be patient and compassionate with yourselves, that some sacrifices are better than others, that you need not wait for a golden ticket to be happy. Please never forget that the *why* of the gospel of Jesus Christ will inspire and uplift you. And never forget that your Heavenly Father knows, loves, and cherishes you.

hank you for who you are. Thank you for the countless acts of love and service you offer up to so many. Thank you for all that you will yet do to bring the joy of the gospel of Jesus Christ to families, to the Church, to your communities, and to the nations of the world.

We love you.

IT IS MY PRAYER AND BLESSING THAT YOU WILL

NEVER FORGET THAT YOU ARE TRULY PRECIOUS

DAUGHTERS IN GOD'S KINGDOM.

NOTES

1. See Ether 12:27.

2. See 3 Nephi 12:48.

3. Roald Dahl, *Charlie and the Chocolate Factory* (New York: Knopf, 1964), 55–56.

4. Articles of Faith 1:13.

5. Psalm 8:3–5.

PRESIDENT DIETER F. UCHTDORF has served as the Second Counselor in the First Presidency of The Church of Jesus Christ of Latter-day Saints since February 3, 2008. He was sustained as a member of the Quorum of the Twelve Apostles in October 2004. He became a General Authority in April 1994 and served as a member of the Presidency of the Seventy from August 2002 until his call to the Twelve.

Prior to his calling as a General Authority, President Uchtdorf was the senior vice president of flight operations and chief pilot of Lufthansa German Airlines.

President Uchtdorf was born in 1940 in what is now the Czech Republic. He grew up in Zwickau, Germany, where his family joined the Church in 1947. He and his wife, Harriet Reich Uchtdorf, are the parents of two children and have six grandchildren.

ISBN-13: 978-1-60907-119-6

SKU 5079600 USD $14.99